WHEN LIFE NEEDS A STICKY NOTE

words of inspiration during challenging times

WAYNE KERR, DDS, MAGD

Ten Tips to the Top!
A primer for the successful dental practice.

BIG Success for Small Business
...a primer for the entrepreneur

When Mom and Dad Need Help...
caring for parents and loved ones

Wise Words
...from Lessons Learned

It's Okay to be Square...
and other wise platitudes

TABLE *of* CONTENTS

PREFACE

Isn't it great to cross an item off a to-do list and enjoy that sense of satisfaction and accomplishment? And aren't sticky notes a useful reminder for jotting down a yet to be completed task? But how about using sticky notes – posted throughout our homes and business – to remind us of what is truly important in our lives?

In times of crisis we can choose to live with an attitude of abundance or scarcity. Choose abundance, and post notes to remind yourself to eliminate your "stinkin' thinkin'" and focus on what's positive. You'll feel better, be healthier, and will emerge more resilient than ever!

This book is a compilation of inspirational essays written after I retired from a busy, small-town practice for general dentistry, and is designed to help you overcome your challenges and emerge as a stronger person, better employer or employee, more loving spouse or parent, and a more valuable member of your community. Be ready to post your own meaningful words on some sticky notes after reading this commentary. Thanks for reading… I wish you the very best.

— *Wayne Kerr, DDS, MAGD*

CHAPTER 1

Live Within Your Means

"There is nothing more uncommon than common sense."

FRANK LLOYD WRIGHT

It troubles me that many young practitioners incur unnecessary debt by buying more than they need to establish their practice. They should begin with the basics and add the bells and whistles as the practice grows. My first office was quite modest and furnished with secondhand equipment. It wasn't much, but it's what I could afford, and it served as the foundation for my ultimate success.

I'm reminded of a memorable weekend of boating, fishing, and camping with Dad and my brother during the mid-sixties. We departed Florida's southwest coast for the Ten Thousand Islands in Dad's old 16′ plywood fishing boat driven by a used Evinrude 40 horsepower outboard. It wasn't much, but it's what we could afford.

One of Dad's friends joined us for the weekend and proudly ran rings around our boat with his 25′ fiberglass ski boat powered by twin 65 Mercs. I suppose I should have been embarrassed, but instead felt like the luckiest kid on the planet as we embarked on this grand adventure.

By late afternoon, we put away the fishing gear and selected a suitable island for the overnight camp. We pan fried the day's catch, pitched our bedrolls, told silly stories, and slept under a billion stars. As the sun awakened us the next morning, however, we discovered that the tide had gone out leaving the beautiful new Merc 65's ruined, buried eighteen inches in the sand. It seems that Dad's friend had forgotten to raise the outboards before securing his boat for the night.

It was a long, slow tow back to the coast, and took most of the day. Our old forty horsepower Evinrude strained at its burden, and finally quit within sight of the dock. Dad got us the rest of the way with our back-up emergency Johnson five horsepower kicker and a couple of paddles. Amazing!

I remember being so proud of my dad that day. He felt genuinely sorry for his friend and was happy to help get him and his boat safely to shore. It didn't matter that our boat wasn't fancy or new. What mattered was that Dad knew what to do and how to do it, and made the most of what he had. So can you.

Dear Reader:

Your turn! Here's a sticky note.
Write your own comment and post

CHAPTER 2

On Building Wealth

"A penny saved is a penny earned."

BENJAMIN FRANKLIN

*Author's Note: Saving even
small sums of money early
in life makes an enormous
impact over time. The key is
to identify sources of savings
and get started. This post is
from May, 2018.*

Some years ago, while presenting "Stuff Worth Knowin' About Money, Practice, and Life" at a national meeting, I observed eight young ladies in matching uniforms walk out shortly after my introduction. I thought perhaps they discovered that they were in the wrong room, but they returned ten minutes before the end of my program toting bags filled with stuffed animals, tooth- brushes, and other goodies from the exhibit hall. I remember thinking at the time, that, if they had just waited ten minutes, they'd have learned how to become financially secure and enjoy a life filled with choices instead of freebies.

That reminded me of a conversation I had with one of my patients some years ago. She had just graduated from high school and became employed by one of our local banks. I congratulated her and suggested that she could now put some money away for her future. She surprised me, however when she complained that she didn't earn enough money to put anything aside.

I asked her if she drank the coffee offered by the bank to its customers and employees. She replied that she bought hers at Starbucks each morning on the way in. Asking what that cost, she advised me that it was about four bucks a cup. I asked her if she brought her lunch from home, only to learn that she "dined out" to get away from work, and that she spent about six dollars every day.

When I pointed out that she was spending some fifty dollars each week on elective purchases, and that she could easily save some money simply by changing her spending habits, she just stared at me. But when I observed that saving fifty dollars a week for forty weeks each year would enable her to put $2,000 a year into a Roth IRA, it was clearly a "lightbulb" moment.

The wealth we accumulate throughout life is dependent upon how much we save, how long it's been saved, and the average rate of return on those savings. Increase any factor, and wealth increases as well. Saving even a little bit early in life, then, makes an incredible impact over time.

If you've never figured out how to save for the future, carefully assess your current spending and develop a realistic budget. Allow for fun, but make some small sacrifices now to secure your ultimate financial freedom. You can do it!

Here's a sticky note:

Post a small change you plan to make in spending.

CHAPTER 3

Share a Smile

"Good vibes are contagious."

FROM "LIFE IS GOOD,
SIMPLE WORDS FROM JAKE AND ROCKET"

Author's Note: It costs nothing
to greet one another with a
smile but doing so can lift
another's spirits and add joy to
their life. Not only does smiling
bring out the best in us, but I
believe it brings out the best in
others as well. The following
post is from March, 2020.

Years before we had cell phones and airline apps, I became aware that my flight from Seattle to Atlanta had been cancelled due to mechanical issues only after arriving at the airport. I wasn't concerned, however, as my airline offered five more Atlanta-bound flights through the course of the day.

The problem I encountered was that I was in a long line with dozens of passengers who had just completed an Alaskan cruise who were also trying to rebook their flights home. By the time I reached the service counter, it was clear that the agent who would help me had been crying. Her hair was a mess, her mascara had run, and she looked rather distraught.

As I handed her my boarding pass and license, I said, "I am so sorry you are not having a good day, and I know it's not your fault that my airplane is broken. I also know that your airline's principle concern is my safety." She just looked at me as though I was speaking a foreign language. Then I said, "I see that you have five more flights today to Atlanta. If you can get me a seat on any one of those, that would be great. I'll even sit in the middle seat of the last row next to the toilet!" And, after saying all this, I offered her a great big smile. I'm sure she thought I was a most peculiar man, but she returned my smile with a small one of her own.

As she turned to her computer, she began to type in various commands. Her actions became faster as she worked to find me a seat and I was impressed with her obvious skill. Ultimately, she printed out a new boarding pass, handed it to me, and said, "Thank you, Mr. Kerr. Have a nice flight," to which I replied, "Thank you so much. I hope your day gets better and better." She surprised me when she said, "Thank you, Sir. It already has."

Leaving the service counter, I headed to the long line at the coffee shop assuming I had hours to kill. That's when I glanced at my boarding pass and discovered that she had booked me on the next flight out and had seated me in first class. Wow! Never underestimate the power of a smile!

Life is better when we choose to smile, even when faced with adversity. It brings out the best in us, and, I believe, helps bring out the best in others. Share a smile and enjoy the moment!

Okay, write a note to post or just draw a "smiley face!"

CHAPTER 4

Choose Your Attitude

There are always flowers for those

who want to see them."

JAKE, FROM "LIFE IS GOOD:
SIMPLE WORDS FROM JAKE AND ROCKET"

When I was eight years old, I joined the Boy Scouts, and looked forward to many adventures, including hiking, camping, and – of course – competing in the soap box derby! I still remember how excited I was to enter my first race and how devastated I was when I finished dead last! The members of my troupe laughed at me, and I cried as I walked home from the meet.

I decided to "get even" with them and quit Scouts. But doing so didn't hurt anyone but me, as I gave up the opportunity to grow as a person through a time-honored youth organization. As I continued to sulk and feel sorry for myself, my father (a former Eagle Scout) invited me to stand in the corner for an hour and consider my attitude. "Be miserable or be happy. It's your life," he said.

I am reminded of an experience that occurred while driving on Florida's turnpike. We were enthusiastically greeted by an employee wearing a Hawaiian shirt at the Wildwood tollway plaza as we traveled south to Orlando. He advised us that, in addition to visiting Disneyworld, we absolutely had to "hit the beach" and see the Kennedy Space Center if we had time. Wahoo!

While leaving the state several days later, we greeted the northbound toll plaza employee with smiles and excited comments about how much fun we'd had while visiting the Sunshine State. I suppose we were "babbling," but he just frowned as he handed us our toll-road entry ticket and told us to "move along." Hmmm...

We all know people who raise our spirits whenever they're around and others who choose to be miserable and spread gloom wherever they go. Some add joy to our lives while others seem to suck the oxygen right out of the air. The difference, of course, is the attitude they've chosen.

Happiness is a function of both thought and action, and is, therefore, within our control. Feeling happy, being grateful, and doing meaningful work enhances our wellness and increases our satisfaction with life. As James M. Barrie said, "Those who bring sunshine to the lives of others cannot keep it from themselves." Clearly, one of the turnpike employees understood that while the other did not.

As my father once wisely advised, "Be miserable or be happy. It's your life!" Let's choose happiness! Life will be longer, healthier, and more fulfilling!

So, does this remind you of an event from your youth? Do you remember sitting in "time out" or standing in the corner? Can you think of a person that brightens the room just by entering it? Write that name on a sticky note with the words "thankful for" under it.

CHAPTER 5

Savor Life's Beauty

"Yesterday is history, tomorrow just a mystery,
but today is a gift, that's why it's called,
the "present."

UNKNOWN

Author's Note: We are surrounded by beauty everyday but rarely pause to appreciate it. Whether it's art, nature, or just a clear, cloudless, cobalt-blue sky, its free for us to enjoy. This post, from February, 2016, is a reminder that, as busy as we are, it's worth pausing from time to time, to savor life's beauty.

Catching up on unread email after returning from an out-of-town lecture, my eyes quickly noted the name of a good friend. Anxious to hear from him, I opened the email only to find that it was the notice of his obituary sent to me by his wife. Having just seen him less than three months ago, I was absolutely stunned!

It was my privilege to attend his funeral service today, as it was not only a last chance for me to say "good-bye," but also to speak comfort to his widow. The service was just like my dear friend: classy and professional, with just the right balance of humor and reverence, music and prayer, celebration and sorrow.

Reflecting on our last office visit together, I remember seeing my good friend uncharacteristically sitting outside the glass door of the office on one of the sofas in our second floor lobby long after his appointment. I took him a bottle of water, and stepped out to see if he needed a ride, was waiting for his wife, or if he needed any help.

He surprised me by saying that he was "taken aback" by the beauty of the turning leaves of our office park's maples, and that the late October afternoon sun had (indeed) brightly illuminated the beautiful (Steffan Thomas) artwork that brings color and class to our open two-story lobby. He said that he just wanted to "sit there," and "take it all in," for we often miss the beauty which surrounds us as we rush through life to meet our responsibilities each day.

We sat together for several minutes in complete silence, absorbed by the brilliant hues of red just outside the glass, the slanted shafts of light, and our thoughts. Before returning to work, I hugged my good friend, and wished him well. As I glanced at him through the closing office door, he was still sitting there, looking very much at peace.

Saying good-bye today reminded me of how fleeting life can be, and of the importance of always valuing our relationships with others. My dear friend lived a great and full life, his loving eulogies a warm afterglow, safe within my heart.

When you close your eyes, what beauty do you see? The face of your spouse, the smile of your child, the stunning colors of azaleas in full bloom? You're gonna need more than one sticky note for this exercise! Use as many as you need, write 'em all down, and post where you can see and enjoy them!

CHAPTER 6

Invest Time in Loved Ones

"I really do believe that all of you are at the beginning of a wonderful journey. As you start traveling down that road of life, remember this: There are never enough comfort stops. The places you're going to are never on the map. And once you get that map out, you won't be able to refold it no matter how smart you are. So forget the map, roll down the windows, and whenever you can, pull over and have a picnic with a pig."

KERMIT THE FROG
"WISDOM FROM IT'S NOT EASY BEING GREEN"

S ometimes we're blessed with such an extraordinary experience, we just can't believe how fortunate we are, nor can we stop smiling! I call them, "Million Dollar Days," because there's no amount of money I'd take in place of the sheer joy I feel in my heart at those special moments and rare occasions! My son-in-law calls them "goose-bump" memories.

Each February I'm privileged to spend ten days in California helping senior dental hygiene students from the west coast prepare for their National Board Exam. This past trip was exceptional in that we traveled up the coast – from Los Angeles to San Francisco - with our "California daughter" and her two children.

We enjoyed absolutely perfect "Chamber of Commerce" weather each day, and shared special adventures, as we drove north on US 1, better known as the Pacific Coast Highway. From the elephant seals just north of San Simeon, to Pfeiffer Beach in Big Sur and beyond to the Golden Gate, each bend in the road – and amazing new vistas – filled us with wonder and a sense of appreciation, as well as childish squeals of delight!

From Big Sur's Ragged Point to the famous wharf of San Francisco, we "crushed" pennies to add to our growing collection of souvenirs! The remarkable "moon" bridge at Golden Gate Park's Japanese Tea Garden enthralled our grandchildren, as each climbed to the top to witness their reflection in the water below. Whether feeding the koi at the Embassy Suites, Brea, or feeding ourselves with a simple road-side picnic, seemingly every activity filled our hearts with joy!

Sometimes we're blessed with such an extraordinary experience, we just can't believe how fortunate we are, nor can we stop smiling! I've been blessed with a generous smattering of "Million Dollar Days" in my life, and am deeply - and humbly -appreciative of each and every one. But now, as I reflect upon the amazing family adventures and experiences of the week gone by, my heart is filled with very special "goose-bump" memories.... For which I am eternally grateful.

This sticky note exercise might require the assistance of the entire family as you revisit and celebrate past adventures. Introduce this as a topic of conversation as you picnic together on the back patio or dine together around the dinner table.

CHAPTER 7

Learn to
Accept Change

*All our dreams can come true if we
have the courage to pursue them."*

WALT DISNEY

Editor's Note: Accepting change is one of the most difficult lessons learned! As spouses, parents, leaders, or small-business owners we must adapt to change, for life IS change. This post was offered in December, 2019.

When our kids were young, we enjoyed many adventures in a small RV. I'd plan detailed itineraries using a few AAA maps and a copy of National Geographic's Guide to the National Parks. Sometimes we'd be on the road for a week or more, exploring the incredible beauty of this great land. Most often, however, we took advantage of long holiday weekends to visit family in Florida and North Carolina.

One favorite trip became an annual event. We'd drive to Pensacola, Florida for the Memorial Day weekend and stay with a relative who lived on the beach. The water was always warm, the sand pristine, the fresh grilled fish delicious, and time together wonderful.

One year, however, circumstances beyond our control prevented us from going, and we were all disappointed. Yes, we'd miss the water, the sand, the food, and time with relatives, but we'd still enjoy the holiday together as a family. And then a crazy thought occurred to me.... What if we pretended that we went?

With a truck load of builder's sand, I converted our backyard pool and patio area into "Pensacola Beach." After spreading the sand appropriately, I put up the big umbrella, broke out the beach chairs, iced down a cooler of soft drinks, and grilled fresh caught salmon. We swam in the pool, batted a beach ball, and played favorite songs by the Beach Boys on a portable CD player. It wasn't quite the same, of course, but feeling the sand between our toes created the desired illusion that we were beach-side and added to the air of festivity!

We can't always do that which we wish to do, but that doesn't mean we should abandon a dream. Want to drive the Pacific Coast Highway, visit New England in the fall, hike Arches National Park, or take a trip on Route 66? Stop wishing! Sit down with a pencil and pad of paper and start planning. List all the reasons why you don't think you can pull it off, and then write down all the reasons why you can. Think creatively, find ways to eliminate the obstacles, and – this year - make it happen. If you don't, no one else will! Happy trails...

It's never too early to plan, especially for something as important as a family outing or adventure! Name the destination, put a date on it, write it on a sticky note and post it where you can see it every day. It's been said that "what gets written gets done." Seeing your dream (or goal) in writing will absolutely help you make it happen!

CHAPTER 8

Develop Coping Strategies

"Never cut a tree down in the wintertime.
Never make a negative decision in the low time.
Never make your most important decisions
when you are in your worst moods. Wait.
Be patient. The storm will pass.
The spring will come."

ROBERT H. SCHULLER

When life presents a challenge that requires a difficult decision, it's important to minimize one's emotional concerns and focus on facts. When logic supersedes emotion, better decisions usually result.

A technique that has worked well for me is to gather as much information as reasonable in the time frame allowed, identify potential advisors, list and compare various options, consult with selected advisors when appropriate, and ultimately determine which option provides the best solution.

If that process sounds intimidating, it's not. Sit down with a legal pad and start writing. What's the issue? What do I know about this? What other information might I need? Who do I know that can assist me? What options do I have?

Give each option its own sheet of paper and divide the sheet vertically into two columns. On the left side, write down all the reasons this option works. On the right side, write down all the reasons this option might not be the best solution. Continue to contribute remarks – pro and con – to each option over a period of days or weeks (depending upon your time-table) as new information becomes available.

When satisfied with the information you've gathered and the assessments you've made, sit down with your team of advisors and review each option. Recognize that no solution may be ideal, but one will likely be better than another. Once you've identified the best option, act to resolve the issue.

This simple problem-solving technique removes the emotional component from the decision-making process while enabling one to compare "apples to apples" by focusing on the facts. The next time you're faced with an insurmountable problem, try this technique. It all just starts with a legal pad and your thoughts.

Although this technique is designed to remove the emotional component from decision-making, don't overlook those family members, friends, or mentors who have provided you invaluable assistance during challenging times. Give them a call, send a note of thanks, or just write their name on a sticky note and post it in their honor!

CHAPTER 9

Let Stuff Go

"Learn from the past without living there, live and grow in the present, and look to the future with hope and optimism."

ZIG ZIGLAR

Remember when you were a kid and couldn't wait until you were old enough to get your driver's license or your first job? And how about high-school graduation? Couldn't come soon enough! "Just wait until…." seemed to be a recurring theme.

Truly, life's early years seemed to last an eternity. Why is it then, that the years seem so much shorter as we age (see my archived blog, "Relatively Speaking…," June, 2015 on kerrspeak.com)? With my fiftieth high school reunion rapidly approaching, I'm left to wonder where has the time gone?

One of the many witticisms my father shared with me was that "life is a journey, not a destination." Not only is that true, but – I believe – it's one of the secrets to loving life. It's one thing to have a childlike wish that Christmas would "hurry up and come," but it's something else to "wish one's life away" while impatiently anticipating the next "big event."

My teammates threw an incredible retirement party for me just before I left clinical practice in 2015. Many former patients attended and were invited to contribute their thoughts on note cards tossed into my "retirement bucket." As much as I appreciated their kind advice and recommendations, I've never had a "bucket list" of things I feel I must accomplish before the opportunity is lost.

By embracing life as a journey, I have cherished each day as the gift that it is (it's called "the present"). Sure, some days have been better than others. Yes, some have brought challenges to be experienced and overcome. But many have been "million-dollar" days that have filled my heart with unimaginable joy.

So, I never bought that Porsche I so desperately wanted, and I sold my beautiful sunburst-finished Gibson acoustical guitar to help pay my college tuition. But I've married the woman of my dreams, held each daughter at birth, given each one away in marriage, and enjoyed an amazing and fulfilling career. I don't need a bucket list to ensure that I have lived life to the fullest, because I already have.

Booker T. Washington once advised that holding a grudge against someone doesn't hurt them, but only the person holding the grudge. Similarly, holding on to the memory of an adverse life-event is destructive. Write down whatever it is, post "I'm letting you go from my life," crumple it up, and toss it. We don't need this sticky note to hang around.

CHAPTER 10

Celebrate Success

"When the week is finally over,
It is wonderful to go
And putter in my garden
Where I watch the flowers grow."
"It is pleasant in my garden
As I cultivate my seeds;
I plant and hoe and water
And I clear away the weeds."
"Though it's frantic at the theater,
Here I leave that all behind,
And the calm within my garden

Gives this frog some peace of mind."

KERMIT THE FROG,
FROM: "IT'S NOT EASY BEING GREEN," BY JIM HENSON

Sometimes it's the little things in life that bring us joy; holding hands with a loved one (without even crossing the street), pausing to appreciate the beauty that surrounds us every day, or watching the colorful display as the sun slips behind the horizon. In the great game of life, however, we often miss these simple joys. Truth be told, we're just too busy.

As the days of December disappear before our very eyes, we're busier than ever! End-of-year administrative responsibilities pile up for the practice owner while patients of record wish to utilize unspent third-party benefits. And, despite the stress, the chaos, and the shortened work schedule, the doctor and his or her staff look forward to well-deserved time off for family and holiday celebrations.

Having experienced this very scenario thirty-five times during my career, I'm reminded of how important it is that we remember to pause, take a breath, and set time aside for quiet reflection. Revisit those experiences which brought you joy, let go of past disappointments you can't change, and fill your heart and mind with those successes which positively impacted the lives of those you serve!

Celebrate who you are, and appreciate that which you and your teammates do for others so effectively, compassionately, and successfully every day! Recognize that you are providing the highest quality of dental health services in history, and that you have remarkable skills that few people on this planet possess.

But, when you're with your family and loved ones, be with your family and loved ones. Focus on the moment, cherish the time together, and celebrate those simple things that often fill your heart with happiness or bring a smile to your lips; maybe the smell of freshly brewed coffee in the morning, the silly family stories shared over dinner, or perhaps the streaking rays of the afternoon sun that illuminate family treasures in the china cabinet. Just little things, really...

In the chaos that is December, let the little things around you bring you happiness and joy, and may your new year be blessed as never before.

No limit on sticky notes here! Get busy, write them down, and enjoy! Wahoo!

Pictures on the Wall

I love art. I'm not sure exactly when in life it became important to me, but it is. The walls of my study are covered with it, and each piece tells a story. Some reflect photos of special moments in family history, some are gifts from friends, and some are purchases made to commemorate meaningful life events.

Having immersed myself into a world of science throughout life, I find that art enhances the quality of it. It introduces a tapestry of rich colors, interesting textures, and a variety of shapes that can lift one's spirits or speak wordlessly to the human soul.

As an engineering student at Georgia Tech, I took graphics my freshman year. Since engineering graphics largely requires drawing straight lines using a T-square, I was extremely disappointed that I earned only a "C" at quarter's end. How is that even possible? Were my ruler-guided lines less straight than others?

As a dental student, however, I quickly came to appreciate that the oral cavity and its structures within, contain no straight lines! By learning to carve the various shapes and contours of teeth, refine the occlusal anatomy and function of each, and establish incisal guidance, freeway space, and the curves of Wilson and Spee, I realized that dentistry truly is a blend of both art and science.

Although I apparently failed to draw straight lines at Georgia Tech, I became empowered with creativity through dentistry. While providing clinical care for thirty-eight years, I carved thousands of wax patterns to be cast into gold restorations and refined the occlusal anatomy of tens of thousands of Class II amalgam and composite fillings. Perhaps that's when I learned to love art.

As I sit in my study composing this blog, I am inspired by the pictures on the walls that surround me, for each piece tells a story. I believe our lives are like a rich tapestry of art, colorfully woven from experiences and events, textured by tragedies and triumphs, and shaped by love, laughter, and achievements.

As your life unfolds, may it be enriched by the pictures on your wall, and may life's experiences bring you a sense of peace, purpose, satisfaction, and joy.

— *Wayne Kerr, DDS, MAGD*

Thanks so much for reading. I hope that these thoughts have inspired and helped you in some small way. And, don't forget, when life needs a sticky note, write down your thoughts and post them. May all your dreams come true...

About the Author

Since 1994, Wayne has been sharing his wit and wisdom with students, educators, and dental professionals across the U. S. and Canada. Although he generally speaks on scientific topics or practice management, his presentations on "Life Skills" seem to resonate with audiences everywhere. His books, *"When Mom and Dad Need Help,"* and *"When Life Needs a Sticky Note"* were written in response to almost universal interest.

"Wise Words from Lessons Learned," was inspired by the many snippets of wisdom offered to Wayne as a youth by his father, J. C. Kerr, Jr. Many of these words of advice contributed to his core values and character, and it is his belief that, by sharing, others can benefit as well. *"It's Okay to be Square"* expands on that theme, and introduces additional concepts embraced by the author.

As a professional, Wayne earned numerous honors, including Fellowship in both the American and International Colleges of Dentistry, the Pierre Fauchard Academy, as an Honored Fellow of the Georgia Dental Association, Mastership in the Academy of General Dentistry, and as a recipient of the Academy's Life Long Learning and Service Recognition Award.

As a community volunteer, Wayne has been recognized as Professional, Citizen, Volunteer, and Small-business Person of the Year. Additionally, he was honored by the Georgia Institute of Technology with its presentation of the Dean Griffin Community Service Award. Working with other community leaders, Wayne helped found a clinic for the indigent providing free dental and medical services.

Retired from clinical care, Wayne's passion is to shorten the learning curve to success for other dentists and their team members. He is an Adjunct Associate Professor for the University of Alabama's School of Dentistry, helps prepare dental hygiene students for their National Board Exam (www.dhseminars.com), speaks on a variety of topics for major dental meetings, and posts a monthly blog called kerrthoughts. Archived blogs are available at www.kerrspeak.com as well as other resources for practice building, or text the word kerrspeak to 22828 to access a link to sign up for his commentary on the first Thursday of every month. Contact Wayne by email at wayne@kerrspeak.com.

Made in the USA
Columbia, SC
24 February 2023

12920959R00050